Collins

English in 5 minutes

Grammar, punctuation and spelling activities

Jon Goulding

CONTENTS

HOW TO USE THIS BOOK

The best way to help your child to build their confidence in English grammar, punctuation and spelling is to give them lots and lots of practice in the key topics and skills.

Written by English experts, this series will help your child master English grammar, punctuation and spelling, and prepare them for SATs.

This book provides ready-to-practise questions that comprehensively cover the English grammar, punctuation and spelling curriculum for Year 4. It contains:

- 36 topic-based tests, each 5 minutes long, to help your child build up their grammar, punctuation and spelling knowledge day-by-day.

- 4 mixed topic tests (Progress Tests), each 5 minutes long, to check progress by covering a mix of topics from the previous 9 tests.

Each test is divided into three Steps:

- **Step 1: Review (1 minute)**
  This exercise helps your child to revise grammar, punctuation and spelling topics they should already know and prepares them for Step 2.

- **Step 2: Practise (2½ minutes)**
  This exercise is a set of questions focused on the topic area being tested.

- **Step 3: Challenge (1½ minutes)**
  This is a more testing exercise designed to stretch your child and deepen their understanding.

Some of the tests also include a Tip to help your child answer questions of a particular type.

Your child should attempt to answer as many questions as possible in the time allowed at each Step. Answers are provided at the back of the book.

To help to measure progress, each test includes boxes for recording the date of the test, the total score obtained, and the total time taken. One mark is awarded for each written part of the answer.

Acknowledgements

The authors and publisher are grateful to the copyright holders for permission to use quoted materials and images.

All images are © HarperCollins*Publishers* Ltd and © Shutterstock.com

Every effort has been made to trace copyright holders and obtain their permission for the use of copyright material. The authors and publisher will gladly receive information enabling them to rectify any error or omission in subsequent editions. All facts are correct at time of going to press.

Published by Collins
An imprint of HarperCollins*Publishers*
1 London Bridge Street
London SE1 9GF

HarperCollins*Publishers*
1st Floor, Watermarque Building,
Ringsend Road, Dublin 4, Ireland

ISBN: 978-0-00-844943-8

First published 2021

10 9 8 7 6 5 4 3 2 1

British Library Cataloguing in Publication Data.

A CIP record of this book is available from the British Library.

Author: Jon Goulding
Publisher: Fiona McGlade
Project Manager: Chantal Addy
Editor: Jill Laidlaw
Cover Design: Kevin Robbins and Sarah Duxbury
Inside Concept Design: Paul Oates and Ian Wrigley
Typesetting Services: Jouve India Private Limited
Production: Karen Nulty
Printed in Great Britain by Martins the Printers

Date: _____

Day of week: _____

> **Tip** *Remember, the **four** main **word classes** are **nouns** (naming people, places or things), **verbs** (action words), **adjectives** (used to describe a noun) and **adverbs** (used to describe a verb). It is important to be able to recognise each of these and understand how they are used in sentences.*

STEP 1 (1 min) Review

Read the passage below. Identify **five nouns** and **seven verbs**, underlining each word class using a different colour.

Mika walked to school slowly. Her large, green bag swung lazily. The daunting school gradually appeared. Mika looked at her beautiful watch. She ran quickly. Luckily, she arrived as the loud bell sounded.

STEP 2 (2.5 min) Practise

Create **two** different sentences which include **one** word from each column of the table below. One example has been done for you.

Nouns	Verbs	Adjectives	Adverbs
crocodile	rolled	wonderful	quickly
Jessica	ate	horrible	gently
car	stopped	dirty	carefully

A dirty car stopped quickly at the junction.

_____

_____

STEP 3 (1.5 min) Challenge

Look at the sentence below. Explain why 'clambered' and 'awkwardly' are better words to use than 'climbed' and 'easily'.

The toddler clambered awkwardly over the rocky wall.

_____

_____

Time spent: _____ min _____ sec. Total: _____ out of 15

Tip *Pronouns* are often used in sentences to replace a *noun*. If a noun is repeated too often in a text, the text becomes less interesting to read. For example: Jake had a red bike. The bike was fast. Jake loved the bike. → Jake had a red bike. It was fast. He loved it.

STEP 1 (1 min) Review

Underline the **pronoun** in each sentence.

Griff walked to school because he lived nearby.

Bobbi is a beautiful dog and she has a fluffy tail.

The cliff was steep and it looked hard to climb.

The brothers were nearly home so they started to run.

STEP 2 (2.5 min) Practise

Add the correct **pronoun** to each sentence.

Mum went to the shops and _____ forgot her purse.

When Dad was ironing, _____ burned his finger.

Jenny's go-kart was fast but _____ was also dangerous.

All of our family went to the beach and _____ had a lovely day.

STEP 3 (1.5 min) Challenge

Read the passage below and replace the highlighted **nouns** with **pronouns** by writing a pronoun in each answer box.

Daisy Dormouse looked cute. **Daisy** was very tiny but **Daisy** was tough. One day,

[   ]   [   ]

the dog found **Daisy** and **the dog** chased **Daisy** around the kitchen. **The kitchen**

[   ]   [   ]   [   ]   [   ]

was a big kitchen and the dog was soon worn out. Daisy managed to give **the dog**

[   ]

a bop on the nose!

3 | Possessive pronouns

Date: _____

Day of week: _____

> **Tip** *Possessive pronouns show ownership of **nouns**. They are used to avoid repetition by replacing a noun when referring to an object belonging to it. For example, Anna likes Oscar's kitten but likes her kitten more. The sentence flows better when 'her kitten' is replaced by 'hers' – Anna likes Oscar's kitten but likes **hers** more.*

STEP 1 (1 min) Review

Underline the **possessive pronoun** in each sentence.

They found some treasure and now it is theirs.

I had a new kite because mine was broken.

I knew that the pencil was not yours.

This bike is better than hers.

STEP 2 (2.5 min) Practise

Complete each sentence with the correct **possessive pronoun**.

Rav and Jazz own a kite.   The kite is _____ .

My bike is great.   The bike is _____ .

You have got a treehouse.   The treehouse is _____ .

Lily likes her new trainers.   The trainers are _____ .

STEP 3 (1.5 min) Challenge

Add the correct **possessive pronoun** to each sentence. Write the **noun** each refers to.

Doug found a newt and says it is now _____.

(_____)

The Smiths won a raffle and say the main prize is now _____.

(_____)

Suzy gave me some cakes which were even tastier than _____.

(_____)

We liked the house but decided _____ is better.

(_____)

Expanded noun phrases

Tip

When you give more information about a noun by using another word such as a determiner and / or an adjective, it becomes a noun phrase. For example, 'the drink' or 'the lovely, cool drink'. Noun phrases can be expanded further. For example, 'the lovely, cool drink in a tall glass'. Here a preposition (in) has been used. Prepositions explain where or when something is happening.

STEP 1 (1 min) Review

Choose a suitable **adjective** or **noun** to modify the **noun phrases** below. Use each word only once.

log	train	summer	hot	cold	bus

She wore a _____ dress.

They stayed in a _____ cabin.

We started our journey from the _____ station.

It was a _____ day.

The _____ carriage was full.

The _____ fire raged.

STEP 2 (2.5 min) Practise

Underline the words which give more information about the highlighted **noun** or **noun phrase** in each sentence.

We saw a wonderful, huge **whale**.

I went on **the ride** next to the rollercoaster.

The autumn wind blew hard.

He wore **a hat** on his head.

STEP 3 (1.5 min) Challenge

Use a **preposition** in each sentence add further information about the **noun**.

I threw my ball _____.

The submarine dived _____.

The snow fell _____.

5 The plural and the possessive 's'

Date: _____

Day of week: _____

> **Tip** *Plural words represent more than one of something, for example, 'two cats', 'these sweets', 'her friends'. Most plurals have an '-s' added to the end of the noun, although some have '-es' ('boxes'), and some words with '-y' endings have the 'y' replaced with 'i' before adding '-es' ('babies'). There are also a number of exceptions (e.g. child → children).*

STEP 1 (1 min) Review

Underline the examples in which an '-**s**' has been added to show a **plural**, and circle examples where the '**s**' has been added to show **possession**.

cricket bats	James lives here
Jayden's haircut	several schools
a large bus	the man's coat
the child's pet	the lovely cats

> **Tip** *The possessive 's' shows that something belongs to someone or something. For singular nouns, an apostrophe followed by 's' is added to the end of the person or thing that is the possessor or owner. For example, Jack's teddy, the school's caretaker.*

STEP 2 (2.5 min) Practise

Rewrite the word from each sentence which should have an **apostrophe**. Write the **plural word** from the sentence next to it.

	Possession	Plural
The chefs apron was full of holes.	_____	_____
Several fireworks fell onto Jamies garden.	_____	_____
The shops manager kept pet snakes.	_____	_____
Dells bus drives around local streets.	_____	_____

STEP 3 (1.5 min) Challenge

Write the correct **plural** for each of the words below:

foxs _____   childs _____   churchs _____

puppys _____   wolfs _____   persons _____

Time spent: _____ min _____ sec. Total: _____ out of 20   ©HarperCollins*Publishers* 2021

| Date: _____ |
| Day of week: _____ |

> **Tip**
>
> *An **adverbial** is used like an adverb to add extra information about a verb, and therefore to the sentence. The adverbial can be a single word or a phrase, for example, They **happily** played football. They played football **all day long**. Sometimes adverbials are used at the beginning of a sentence to provide variety in sentence structure or change the emphasis of the words. For example: **Happily**, they played football. **All day long**, they played football. These are known as **fronted adverbials**. Fronted adverbials describe the action that follows. They often have a comma after them.*

STEP 1 (1 min) Review

Underline the **fronted adverbial** in each sentence.

Slowly and carefully, she climbed the rockface.

On the other side of the playground, Jess hid behind a large shed.

At the back of the bus, Evan was feeling sick.

STEP 2 (2.5 min) Practise

Rewrite each sentence so the underlined adverbial phrase becomes a **fronted adverbial**.

The snow melted <u>within hours</u>.

_____

Everyone ate popcorn <u>during the film</u>.

_____

We built amazing sandcastles <u>using buckets and spades</u>.

_____

STEP 3 (1.5 min) Challenge

Match each **fronted adverbial** with the most suitable ending for the sentence. Rewrite the sentence you make with the adverbial in a different place.

Just in time,   Following the downpour,

_____ the eel managed to squirm away.

_____

_____ fields became huge lakes.

_____

7 Determiners

> **Tip**
>
> *Determiners* are used to give more information about nouns. Remember – 'a' before a consonant (a dog) and **'an'** before a vowel (an egg). Other examples: **this** house, **that** house, **the** house, **a** house, **those** houses. They are also used to suggest **quantities**, for example, **two** houses, **some** houses, **few** houses, **many** houses. Possessive determiners show belonging, for example, **their** house, **our** house, **your** house, **my** house.

STEP 1 (1 min) Review

Underline **two determiners** and the **nouns** they give information about in each sentence.

They watched an eagle circling above those trees.

Molly had heard that sound when she slept in her tent.

As soon as they saw the time, they knew they had missed their bus.

This amazing garden belongs to my family, thought Billy.

STEP 2 (2.5 min) Practise

Circle the correct **determiner** in bold to use in each sentence.

There are **fewer / some / those** people in the UK than in China.

Chrissy ate **a / an / several** apple yesterday.

You can bring the game to **some / those / my** house to play.

Claudia knew that **these / your / an** incredible jewel had been stolen.

At twelve years old, he set up **his / those / an** car-washing business.

STEP 3 (1.5 min) Challenge

Find and replace the **determiner** that has been used incorrectly in each example.

The cat had five kittens. The vet checked every cute kittens were healthy.

_____

_____

Half of the team were off school but there were still lots children to choose from.

_____

_____

Time spent: _____ min _____ sec. Total: _____ out of 15

©HarperCollins*Publishers* 2021

Date: _____

Day of week: _____

 Tip *Conjunctions are used to join different parts of a sentence. They are also used to show when (time) and why (cause) something happened.*

STEP 1 (1 min) Review

Underline the **conjunction** in each sentence. Add a tick to the correct column to show whether it shows cause or time.

Sentence	Cause	Time
Wash your hands before you eat your lunch.		
They were very cold because they were not wearing coats.		
The dog was chewing the cushion while Zak watched television.		
It was a hot day so they took plenty of water with them.		

STEP 2 (2.5 min) Practise

Rewrite each sentence using the **conjunction** as the first word while keeping the meaning the same. A comma follows the part of the sentence containing the conjunction. The first one has been done for you.

You have to go to the jungle, if you ever get the chance.

If you ever get the chance, you have to go to the jungle.
_____

They had to take shelter as the monsoon rain was torrential.

_____

We searched for days for vines and fallen trees so we could make a raft.

_____

The river was wide and fast because the rain had been falling heavily.

_____

STEP 3 (1.5 min) Challenge

Choose the most suitable **conjunction** to add to each sentence.

Because / If / Before _____ they go on their bikes, they must wear helmets.

so / because / when They hid beneath the stairs _____ they played hide and seek.

because / after / if The water was still pouring in _____ the rain had stopped.

Date: _____

Day of week: _____

✏️ **Tip** *Time, cause and place are indicated by **conjunctions**, **adverbs** and **prepositions**.*

STEP 1 (1 min) **Review**

Choose a different adverb from below to complete each sentence. Label each adverb **time**, **place** or **cause**.

because	through	before	since

They had been waiting for the bus _____ 7:30am.   _____

We needed a safety rope _____ we could have fallen.   _____

I looked around and recognised that I'd been here _____.   _____

The traffic stopped to let the train pass _____.   _____

STEP 2 (2.5 min) **Practise**

Read the passage below. All the **prepositions** are in the wrong place. Rewrite the text with each in the correct place.

We all lay in the ground. It was great being through the stars. We could see hundreds of them sparkling under the night sky. Later we looked on the telescope.

_____

_____

_____

STEP 3 (1.5 min) **Challenge**

Write **two** different sentences which include the word '**before**'. In **one** sentence use it as an **adverb** (appearing after the noun) and in the other use it as a **preposition** (appearing before the noun).

adverb

_____

preposition

_____

Time spent: _____ min _____ sec. Total: _____ out of 14   ©HarperCollins*Publishers* 2021

STEP 1 ⏱(1 min) Review

Underline the **first determiner**, the **pronoun** and the **possessive determiner** in each sentence.

Sam saw the eagle first. He quickly picked up his binoculars for a closer look.

That noise hurt our ears. Nobody knew where it came from.

Dana lives in that house. She keeps chickens in her garden.

A large cloud hung above their heads and it got bigger and bigger.

STEP 2 ⏱(2.5 min) Practise

Rewrite the word from each sentence which should have an **apostrophe**. Write the **plural word** from the sentence next to it.

	Possession	Plural
The cathedrals bells rang out.	_____	_____
We ate pizzas at Louies house.	_____	_____
While crossing fields, my shoes sole fell off.	_____	_____
There are bushes all along Miffs driveway.	_____	_____

STEP 3 ⏱(1.5 min) Challenge

Complete the **fronted adverbial**, and the **expanded noun phrase** for each sentence.

While _____ , they saw a _____ nearby.

Beneath the _____ , we wore _____ on

our heads.

Date: _____

Day of week: _____

Tip

*In writing, **tense** is used to reference when an event or events 'took place', 'take place', 'are taking place' or 'will take place'. The **present perfect tense** describes events that 'have happened' before now (the present) without specifying exactly when they happened. For example, They **have been** on holiday.*

STEP 1 (1 min) Review

Complete the table below.

Verb	Simple present	Simple past	Present perfect
I	am		have been
you		were	have been
he / she / it		was	
they	are		

STEP 2 (2.5 min) Practise

Replace the underlined **verbs** in the sentence with the same verbs to show the given tense for that sentence.

We <u>are writing</u> a letter to Grandma. ⬭ past tense

Mum <u>painted</u> a portrait. ⬭ present tense

The rocket <u>is blasting</u> into space. ⬭ present perfect tense

A huge wave <u>crashed</u> into the cliff. ⬭ present tense

STEP 3 (1.5 min) Challenge

Read the eyewitness account telling the television reporter about an ongoing incident at a bank.

Rewrite the account in the **present perfect tense**, using the **verb 'to have'**, and the correct version of the **main verb**, to show these events have happened before now.

The car stopped suddenly. Two people leaped out and charged into the bank. They were in there for two hours now. The police arrived within a few minutes of the situation starting.

_____

_____

_____

Time spent: _____ min _____ sec. Total: _____ out of 15

Tip *Standard English is the 'correct' form of English used around the world. It is used when speaking and writing formally. In Standard English, slang words are not used, and subjects and verbs agree, for example, 'we were' is used rather than 'we was'.*

STEP 1 (1 min) Review

Read each sentence. Circle the **correct form** to use to replace the underlined word.

I <u>ain't</u> got my lunch with me.   **is not / am not / have not**

They <u>was</u> on holiday last week.   **will be / were / wasn't**

Pass me <u>them</u> tools please.   **that / those / this**

They all did <u>good</u> in their spelling test.   **well / best / gooder**

STEP 2 (2.5 min) Practise

Read the text below. Rewrite it, ensuring that **Standard English** is used throughout.

When I were on the train I meeted my old friend. We buyed some lunch and done lots of talking. We has both been working in London. She said she don't like it but I do. In London there is many places to visit. They even has a big wheel called the London Eye.

_____

_____

_____

_____

STEP 3 (1.5 min) Challenge

Write **two** sentences related to the picture. In the first sentence use '**am**' and '**are**' correctly, and in the second sentence use '**was**' and '**were**' correctly.

_____

_____

_____

_____

Date: _____

Day of week: _____

Tip *Commas can be used to separate items in a list and to separate some clauses in sentences. A comma is often placed after a fronted adverbial.*

STEP 1 (1 min) Review

Add **commas** to the lists below.

Emmy bought eggs flour butter and milk to make pancakes.

_____

Sam's top three toppings are chocolate spread banana and lemon juice.

_____

Everyone was told to bring cakes old toys books and sweets for the school sale.

_____

STEP 2 (2.5 min) Practise

Underline the fronted adverbial in each sentence and add a **comma** in the correct place.

As quickly as possible they ran towards the station.

After their delicious lunch everybody needed a snooze.

Down at the harbour Joss could see a huge sailing ship.

Looking at the wonderful scene Kat remembered the last time she was there.

In the shade of the oak tree the whole class sat and dozed.

Carefully and silently Lily reached for the next rope.

STEP 3 (1.5 min) Challenge

Explain the mistake in each sentence below.

During the long, film Matty fell asleep.

_____

We saw, lions, tigers, elephants, giraffes and gorillas.

_____

Time spent: _____ min _____ sec. Total: _____ out of 19

©HarperCollins*Publishers* 2021

Date: _____

Day of week: _____

Tip There are **four** main sentence types: *statements, commands, questions* and *exclamations*. Using a variety of sentence types in writing not only makes it more interesting for the reader but also makes writing more precise.

STEP 1 (1 min) Review

Match each sentence to the **sentence type**. Add the **correct punctuation** to the end of each sentence.

statement	command	question	exclamation
What an incredible meal they were served	They waited to be seated at the restaurant	Wash your hands before eating, please	What food would you recommend

STEP 2 (2.5 min) Practise

Write a **statement**, a **command** and a **question** using each given word.

socks _____

_____

_____

swim _____

_____

_____

STEP 3 (1.5 min) Challenge

Change each given sentence into a different type of **sentence**. Change or add any words as necessary.

Pass me my pencil.

_____

How fantastic it is to see you!

_____

Do you know where I put my keys?

_____

Date: _____

Day of week: _____

Tip *A clause is part of a sentence. A sentence can be a **single-clause** sentence, or a **multi-clause** sentence. Each clause must contain a **verb**. In a sentence, there will be at least one main clause (a clause which makes sense on its own) for example, 'the bread was mouldy'. There can be further main clauses and / or **subordinate clauses** (clauses which do not make sense on their own, for example, 'because it was old').*

STEP 1 (1 min) **Review**

Write **M** for **main clause** or **S** for **subordinate clause** after each clause below.

when the rain started ____

they looked at the giant creature ____

the cake tasted delicious ____

so they had more ____

STEP 2 (2.5 min) **Practise**

Underline the **main clauses** and circle the **subordinate clauses** in these sentences.

The dog was asleep when the cat was awake.

We built a snowman because snow had covered the garden.

While they were swimming somebody hid their shoes.

We will go the art gallery if the museum is closed.

STEP 3 (1.5 min) **Challenge**

Add a **main clause** or **subordinate clause** to each of the clauses below.

Rishi saw the smoke _____

As the river flowed _____

A glorious sun was rising _____

When they arrived _____

Time spent: _____ min _____ sec. Total: _____ out of 16   ©HarperCollins*Publishers* 2021

Tip Direct speech refers to the words spoken by a person in a story or other text. The actual words that are spoken are placed within inverted commas, also known as speech marks.

STEP 1 1 min Review

Read the passage below. Underline the **direct speech** – the actual words that are being spoken.

It was a dull day. I wish this rain would pass, moaned Milly. She did not like riding her bike in the rain. Only three more miles until the café, said Mum encouragingly. Despite the rain, Milly now pushed harder on the pedals. She thought of chocolate cake. Almost joyfully she shouted, Come on, I'll race you.

STEP 2 2.5 min Practise

Add **inverted commas** in the correct places in each sentence.

Can we have lunch yet? asked Seb.

We will stop in 20 minutes, replied Ali.

Her tummy rumbling, Jess said, I am so, so hungry. I need food.

We'll stop at the top of this hill as the views are wonderful, promised Ali.

STEP 3 1.5 min Challenge

Explain what other **punctuation** is needed for **direct speech** by looking at the example below.

"Has Charlie finished?" asked Dad.

"Yes, he's done a great job tidying his room," said Mum.

_____

_____

Date: _____

Day of week: _____

> **Tip**
> As well as ensuring **direct speech** is within speech marks (inverted commas), additional punctuation is needed. The spoken words are separated from the *reporting clause* (which says who spoke and often how they spoke) by **commas, question marks, or exclamation marks.** For example, "How are you today?" asked Sam. Because the spoken words are a question, a question mark is used to help indicate this. The question mark is part of the spoken words, so is within the inverted commas. The reporting clause ends with a full stop.

STEP 1 (1 min) Review

Tick the **two** sentences that are punctuated correctly.

"It's time to go. Hurry!" shouted Gran. ☐

"You are a really good runner, said Lena." ☐

"Can I have a go, please," asked Jamie? ☐

Lizzie asked, "Who would like to play?" ☐

STEP 2 (2.5 min) Practise

Add the missing punctuation to each example of **direct speech.**

Please walk carefully as the floor is wet said the cleaner.

Are you going on holiday asked the bus driver.

When Chloe saw the car, she screamed Look out

You have five tasks today said the teacher.

STEP 3 (1.5 min) Challenge

Using the information below, turn each sentence into **direct speech.**

Tommy asked if he could go on a bike ride.

_____

Emma told her sister she would help her with her homework.

_____

Time spent: _____ min _____ sec. Total: _____ out of 13

Date: _____

Day of week: _____

Tip *Apostrophes are commonly used to show **contraction** (when two words are pushed together to make a shorter word) for example, do not → don't, you will → you'll. The apostrophe takes the place of the missing letter(s).*

STEP 1 (1 min) Review

Write each word containing the **apostrophe** in the correct place in the table.

you can't go   Lena's drink

the cow's grass   who would've thought

Jess's diary   we won't be there

a book's cover   you'll soon find out

Tip *Apostrophes are also used to show **possession** – when an object belongs to someone or something. For example, Mum's motorbike – the apostrophe and 's' ('s) after Mum, shows that the motorbike belongs to her. If the 'owner' already ends in 's' then it is acceptable to use just an apostrophe placed after that 's' (s') although for proper nouns 's can still be added, for example, James's school bag.*

Apostrophe for contraction	Apostrophe for possession

STEP 2 (2.5 min) Practise

Use the correct form of the **apostrophe** for contraction or possession in each example below.

We saw the _____ toy in the garden.   [toy belonging to the cat]

The horse goes inside if _____ raining.   [it is]

The _____ wheel fell off.   [the wheel of the bus]

STEP 3 (1.5 min) Challenge

Write a sentence that uses the possessive **apostrophe** for each given idea.

a guitar belonging to Thomas

_____

a painting belonging to Alisha

_____

Date: _____

Day of week: _____

Tip

*When nouns become plural (representing more than one) they often have an 's' added to the end of the word, for example, 'horses' – more than one horse. When showing possession for plural nouns already ending in 's', the **apostrophe** is added **after the 's' (s')**, for example, 'the horses' stable' – a stable belonging to more than one horse, 'the foxes' den' – the den belonging to more than one fox. For plural nouns which do not end in 's', an **apostrophe followed by 's'** is added to the word to show possession, for example, 'the men's changing room'.*

STEP 1 (1 min) Review

Write **P** or **S** on the line to show whether the underlined noun is **plural** or **singular**.

We caught hold of the <u>ropes</u> which hung from the tree.   _____

Nobody knew if the <u>boys</u> would find their way in the dark.   _____

The blue <u>bus</u> went to the airport.   _____

STEP 2 (2.5 min) Practise

Underline the **possessive noun** in each sentence. Write **SP** or **PP** for singular possession or plural possession.

The car's engine sounded awful.   _____

Nine children's playgrounds have been closed.   _____

It is difficult to change people's beliefs.   _____

The fox's cubs played in the snow.   _____

The wreck got caught in the fishermen's nets.   _____

STEP 3 (1.5 min) Challenge

Explain the difference in the position of the **apostrophe** in the underlined words below.

The <u>witches'</u> brooms flew them to the place where the golden <u>geese's</u> eggs lay.

_____

_____

Time spent: _____ min _____ sec. Total: _____ out of 15   ©HarperCollinsPublishers 2021

Date: _____

Day of week: _____

STEP 1 (1 min) Review

Rewrite each sentence, changing the **verb** to ensure **Standard English** is used.

Fish and chips is nice together.

_____

Jess don't like swimming.

_____

The crowd were huge at the concert.

_____

The plates was in the dishwasher.

_____

STEP 2 (2.5 min) Practise

Rewrite each sentence, ensuring **apostrophes** are added for **possession** where needed, and for **contraction** of the underlined words.

The childrens club <u>has not</u> been open for weeks.

_____

James homework <u>will not</u> be finished on time.

_____

You <u>should not</u> eat Sophies sweets.

_____

<u>We are</u> going to my friends house for lunch.

_____

STEP 3 (1.5 min) Challenge

Rewrite each sentence below, ensuring the **punctuation** is correct.

"Chloe shouted It's a clown!"

_____

Where are the car keys "asked Dad."

_____

21 | Prefixes

STEP 1 (1 min) Review

Add a **prefix** (a letter or letters placed before a word to change the meaning) to each of the words below and write them in the correct columns in the table.

mature	usual	appear	possible	understood
advantage	fashionable	perfect	tidy	agree	behave

Prefix 'dis-'	Prefix 'mis-'	Prefix 'un-'	Prefix 'im-'

STEP 2 (2.5 min) Practise

Underline each word in the text below which has an **incorrect prefix**. Write the correct words in the spaces provided.

The restaurant was very misorganised. Some people became dispatient as they found the service unadequate. The manager seemed highly inresponsible, as he kept letting more people in. This was quite imlogical as all the tables were full. For most, the experience was inperfect.

_____ _____ _____

_____ _____ _____

STEP 3 (1.5 min) Challenge

Write a definition for each of the words below. In the definition, explain what the **prefix** means. Use your dictionary to help you.

international

_____

replay

_____

Time spent: _____ min _____ sec. Total: _____ out of 19

Date: _____

Day of week: _____

Tip *Suffixes can be added to the end of root words to change their meaning.*

STEP 1 (1 min) Review

Match each word to the most suitable **suffix**, and then write the new word. Use each suffix once.

joyous   -ful   _____

enjoy   -ment   _____

care   -ed   _____

race   -ly   _____

STEP 2 (2.5 min) Practise

Explain what changes need to be made to each word below when the given **suffix** is added.

When adding '-ly' to 'happy'

_____

When adding '-ing' to 'face'

_____

When adding '-ment' to 'merry'

_____

STEP 3 (1.5 min) Challenge

Add the **'-ly'** suffix to each of the words below, ensuring any other changes required to the word ending are also made.

basic _____

gentle _____

angry _____

historic _____

Time spent: _____ min _____ sec. Total: _____ out of 15

Date: _____

Day of week: _____

STEP 1 (1 min) Review

Rewrite each sentence using the highlighted word with the **'-ly' suffix**.

A storm is approaching and it's coming **quick**.

_____

They waited for lunch **silent**.

_____

STEP 2 (2.5 min) Practise

Group the words below into different columns in the table by adding the **suffix '-ous'**. In the first row of each column, write a rule to explain what has happened to the root word when adding '**-ous**'. The first one has been done for you.

envy	rigour	fame	humour	nerve	victory

'y' ending changed to 'i' before adding '-ous'		
envious		

STEP 3 (1.5 min) Challenge

Write the correct word (with the correct **suffix**) for each highlighted root word in the passage below.

Jasper chased the cat **rapid** (_____) around the garden. The grass was wet and the **run** (_____) animals were making it muddy. The children joined in – they **prefer** (_____) to be outside in the mud. Soon everyone was tired and when they **notice** (_____) it **become** (_____) dark, they **tap** (_____) on the door so Mum could let them in.

Date: _____

Day of week: _____

Tip   *The suffix '-ation' can be added to some verbs to make a noun.*

STEP 1 (1 min) Review

Match each **noun** to its meaning.

population	**operation**	**narration**	**relaxation**
The reading of a story	The easing of something or taking it easy	An organised activity	The number of something living somewhere

STEP 2 (2.5 min) Practise

Rewrite each highlighted word with the addition of the **suffix '-ation'**.

Their **prepare** for the trip was very thorough. _____

There would have to be a thorough **investigate** of the crime. _____

An incredible rock **form** rose from the desert floor. _____

Much more **inform** was needed before they could take the challenge. _____

All the children worked hard to create the **animate**. _____

She felt a strange **sense** when she walked into the room. _____

STEP 3 (1.5 min) Challenge

Explain what changes need to be made when '**-ation**' is added to the words below.

admire _____

_____

occupy _____

_____

exclaim _____

_____

Date: _____

Day of week: _____

Tip Adding the **suffix '-ous'** to a noun changes it into an **adjective**. For example, danger → *dangerous*. Sometimes the ending of the root word changes before adding '-ous' as in the verb vary → *various*.

STEP 1 (1 min) Review

Circle the words which can have the **suffix '-ous'** added and write the new words underneath.

fame   luck   murder

mountain   regular   fruit

_____

STEP 2 (2.5 min) Practise

Complete each word, using the clues to help.

__ u __ r a __ __ __ __ s   When something causes outrage.

p __ __ c __ __ u __   Something with value to someone.

b __ i __ t e __ o __ __   Loud behaviour.

__ __ s t e r i __ __ __   Something strange.

STEP 3 (1.5 min) Challenge

Explain what changes need to be made to the words below when the **suffix '-ous'** is added. Use a dictionary to help you.

miracle   _____

          _____

mischief   _____

          _____

Time spent: _____ min _____ sec. Total: _____ out of 9   ©HarperCollins*Publishers* 2021

Date: _____

Day of week: _____

Tip *In some words, the short 'i' sound, as represented by 'i' in the word 'sit', is replaced by a 'y'. These words just have to be learned.*

STEP 1 (1 min) Review

Underline each word in the text below, in which the short 'i' sound is represented by 'y'. Write each word in the spaces provided.

Last year we visited Egypt. It was fantastic. We saw the pyramids and learned all about these mysterious structures. It was not a typical holiday but it was great fun.

_____   _____

_____   _____

STEP 2 (2.5 min) Practise

Complete each word below, using the clues to help. Use a dictionary too, if needed.

g __ __   A place where people exercise.

s __ n o __ __ m   A word with the same or similar meaning to another.

c __ g n e __   A baby swan.

m __ __ t e r __   Something that cannot be explained.

STEP 3 (1.5 min) Challenge

Complete each sentence with the appropriate word, using 'y' for the short 'i' sound.

In maths, we often use the s_____ '+' and '−' for addition and subtraction.

During church services, people sing h_____.

S_____ is a sweet sticky substance we can put on pancakes.

When we breathe, we use o_____ from the air.

Our school has a new computer s_____.

Date: _____

Day of week: _____

Tip *The 'ch' spelling can make a 'sh' sound as represented by 'sh' in 'shop'. This spelling is borrowed from French. 'ch' can also make the 'k' sound as in 'kitten'. This spelling has its origins in Greek.*

STEP 1 (1 min) Review

Write the words below in the correct column in the table.

| chef | ache | chauffeur | chaos | character | moustache |

'ch' making a 'sh' sound	'ch' making a 'k' sound

STEP 2 (2.5 min) Practise

Read each clue and write the correct word containing 'ch' from the list below.

| school | chorus | mechanic | anchor | chemist | machine |

Used to stop ships drifting at sea. _____

A mechanical tool used for making things. _____

A repeating part of a song. _____

A person who works with chemicals. _____

A place of education. _____

A person who fixes things such as cars. _____

STEP 3 (1.5 min) Challenge

Underline the **nine** words in which 'ch' makes a 'sh' sound or a 'k' sound.

During the school play, the chemistry teacher changed the position of the smoke machine and there was chaos. The main character could not be seen and the joke about the moustache was missed. The person playing the chauffeur missed his entrance and was munching on a crunchy apple instead of serving champagne and quiche onstage to the leading lady.

Time spent: _____ min _____ sec. Total: _____ out of 21

Tip The 'gue' and 'que' spelling pattern in words has its origins in the French language. 'gue' at the end of a word sounds like the sound represented by 'g' in the word 'gone'. 'que' at the end of a word sounds like the sound represented by 'k' in the word 'weak'.

STEP 1 (1 min) Review

Match each definition to the correct word.

Something old such as an old clock   boutique

A fancy shop   picturesque

A method or way of doing something   antique

A beautiful scene or setting   technique

STEP 2 (2.5 min) Practise

Underline the words in the passage below which use the '**que**' and '**gue**' spellings borrowed from French. Write the words in the spaces provided. Write the meaning of each word you find.

On the way home from the mosque, Naveed saw his colleague from their unique shop. Despite a long day and feeling fatigued, they stood and chatted for ages. They needed to discuss the new catalogue which they would use for selling intriguing items of art.

_____   _____

_____   _____

_____   _____

_____   _____

_____   _____

_____   _____

STEP 3 (1.5 min) Challenge

The letters '**pla**' can have both '**que**' and '**gue**' added to them. Write the words and find **two** definitions for each. Use a dictionary to help you.

pla_____   _____

_____

pla_____   _____

The 'sc' spelling from Latin

Date: _____

Day of week: _____

Tip

Some words beginning with an 's' sound use the letters 'sc'. This spelling originates from the Latin language. The same spelling pattern is sometimes found within words too. In ancient times it is possible that the 's' and 'c' were sounded in the same way as the 'sk' is in the word 'sky'. This is sometimes a useful way of remembering how to spell these words.

STEP 1 (1 min) Review

Match each definition below to the correct word.

scimitar   **science**   **disciple**   **crescent**

A follower of a leader, such as Jesus	A type of sword	A curved moon shape	The study and investigation of the natural world

STEP 2 (2.5 min) Practise

Read the passage below. Circle the words that have been spelt incorrectly and write the correct spellings in the spaces underneath.

Kian reached for the sissors. He wanted to cut out the picture of the mountain sene. For years he had been fasinated by mountains and he dreamed of asending this one. He knew it would not be easy – he was a sientist and he knew such a climb would test his musles to their limits.

_____   _____   _____

_____   _____   _____

STEP 3 (1.5 min) Challenge

Look at the three words below.

| scent   ascent   descent |

Which word is the odd one out and what does it mean?

_____

Explain the similarities and differences between the other two words.

_____

Time spent: _____ min _____ sec. Total: _____ out of 12   ©HarperCollins*Publishers* 2021

Date: _____

Day of week: _____

STEP 1 (1 min) Review

Correct the spelling of each of the words below.

mistery _____   piramid _____

gimnasium _____   oxigen _____

himn _____   tipical _____

STEP 2 (2.5 min) Practise

Complete the sentences with appropriate words starting with or containing '**sc**', '**gue**' or '**que**'.

In our **s**_____ lesson, we learned about changes.

The old ornament in our living room is an **a**_____.

Gran made us a lemon **m**_____ pie for dessert.

A narrow **c**_____ of moon hung in the night sky.

My uncle plays golf with his **c**_____ from work.

A **m**_____ is an Islamic place of worship.

STEP 3 (1.5 min) Challenge

For each word below, write the **root word** and then the word with the **suffix '-ation'** added.

	Root word	+ '-ation'
narrative	_____	_____
forming	_____	_____
sensitive	_____	_____
operational	_____	_____

Time spent: _____ min _____ sec. Total: _____ out of 20

31 '-sure' endings

> **Tip** The **'-sure'** ending at the end of the word **'treasure'** has a distinct sound that can be distinguished from the sound made by the same spelling in words such as **'sure'** and **'reassure'**.

STEP 1 (1 min) Review

Place a tick next to the words which have the same final sound as '**treasure**'.

fresher ☐   pressure ☐

pleasure ☐   feature ☐

teacher ☐   measure ☐

richer ☐   closure ☐

STEP 2 (2.5 min) Practise

Choose the correct word to add to each sentence. Use a dictionary to help.

enclosure	treasure	leisure	erasure

After accidental _____ of the computer data, all the lessons were

mixed up.

In their _____ time they enjoy surfing and swimming.

Some buildings and places are considered to be a national _____.

Safari park patrols ensure that all animals are in their _____.

STEP 3 (1.5 min) Challenge

Write the meaning of each of the words below. Use a dictionary to help.

composure_____

_____

disclosure _____

_____

Time spent: _____ min _____ sec. Total: _____ out of 9   ©HarperCollins*Publishers* 2021

Date: _____

Day of week: _____

Tip *Many words ending in a '-cher' sound as in 'teacher' have the letters '-ture' at the end.*

STEP 1 (1 min) Review

Match each definition to the correct word.

Everything natural   creature

A large bird of prey   vulture

A living animal   fracture

A break in something   nature

STEP 2 (2.5 min) Practise

Use the words given below to complete each section of text. Use a dictionary to help you.

capture	feature	picture	structure	sculpture	furniture

They lived in an apartment in the largest _____ in town. Their

_____ was all handmade and they had an indoor pond – a rather

interesting _____ to have in the middle of the living room.

On the wall hung a beautiful _____ of a sunset. The artist had

managed to _____ the light perfectly. Next to the pond stood an

incredible glass _____ of a flower.

STEP 3 (1.5 min) Challenge

Give each word a '-ture' ending and write a sentence containing that word.

mix_____ _____

depart_____ _____

moist_____ _____

Date: _____

Day of week: _____

Tip *Many words have endings that sound like 'shun', as in 'station'. Words ending in the spelling patterns '-tion', '-cian', '-sion' and '-ssion' make the same sound. '-tion' is most common if the root word ends in 't' or 'te', '-ssion' if the root word ends in 'ss' or 'mit', '-sion' replaces 'd' or 'se' endings and '-cian' replaces 'c' or 'cs' endings.*

STEP 1 (1 min) Review

Match each definition to the correct word.

What pupils receive at school   musician

Somebody who plays in a band   action

A newly thought of thing   education

Something being done   invention

STEP 2 (2.5 min) Practise

Add the correct **'shun' ending** to each of the words below. Use a dictionary to help you.

attend _____

complete _____

discuss _____

tense _____

expand _____

magic _____

STEP 3 (1.5 min) Challenge

Explain what changes need to be made when adding the **'-ion'** ending to the words **'admit'**, **'permit'** and **'transmit'**.

_____

_____

Time spent: _____ min _____ sec. Total: _____ out of 11   ©HarperCollins*Publishers* 2021

Tip 'zhun' endings *make the sound heard at the end of the word* **'division'**. *This ending is often used to turn verbs ending in* **'-se'** *or* **'-de'** *into nouns.*

STEP 1 (1 min) Review

Choose the correct word from below to add to each sentence.

illusion	vision	collision	decision

There was a terrible _____ when the two drivers did not see each other.

The headteacher came to a fair _____ about the new school uniform.

At the magic show, the magician demonstrated an amazing _____.

Some creatures have incredible _____.

STEP 2 (2.5 min) Practise

Change each of the nouns below to verbs. Use a dictionary to help you with your spelling.

Noun	Verb
revision	_____
confusion	_____
intrusion	_____
invasion	_____
television	_____
erosion	_____

STEP 3 (1.5 min) Challenge

Sort the words below into three groups based on the word endings. Think of a title for each group.

conclusion   extension   profession   mansion   procession   explosion

_____	_____	_____

Date: _____

Day of week: _____

Tip The letter patterns 'ei', 'eigh', and 'ey' can make a long 'a' sound as represented by the a–e in the words game, mane, late, wade and cape.

STEP 1 (1 min) Review

Complete the words in each sentence with the correct letters to represent the long 'a' sound.

They got in trouble for disob__ __ ing the teacher.

My great-grandad celebrated his __ __ __ __ tieth birthday.

We had to w__ __ __ __ the fruit before we paid for it.

The bride wore a beautiful white v__ __ l.

STEP 2 (2.5 min) Practise

The following words have been spelt using the wrong long 'a' sound. Spell them correctly, then write a sentence containing each word.

naybour _____ _____

thay _____ _____

raindeer _____ _____

greigh _____ _____

STEP 3 (1.5 min) Challenge

What is the difference in meaning between these two words with the long 'a' sound?

prey and **pray**

_____

_____

Time spent: _____ min _____ sec. Total: _____ out of 14

Date: _____

Day of week: _____

Tricky words (1) 36

Tip *There are many words which have **tricky spellings**. This can sometimes mean they are tricky to say too. These words just have to be learned.*

STEP 1 (1 min) Review

Each word below has a common silent letter. Underline the **silent letter** in each word.

build   **tongue**   **favourite**   **guilty**

Choose the **two** words from above to complete the sentence below.

Her _____ time at school was when they were allowed to get the

construction toys out and _____ whatever they wanted.

STEP 2 (2.5 min) Practise

Complete each sentence with the correct word below.

question	guards	guide	antique

The _____ took them on a tour of the castle. In one special

room they saw the _____ diamonds and gold rings. Somebody

asked a _____ about security. The guide said there were

_____ there all day and night.

STEP 3 (1.5 min) Challenge

What **sound** does the letter '**u**' make in 'busy'?

_____

Add the **endings** below to the word 'busy'. Write the new words.

-est _____

-ness _____

Date: _____

Day of week: _____

Tip *In many words containing a 'c', this letter makes an 's' sound.*

STEP 1 (1 min) **Review**

Underline all of the '**s**' **sounds** in the words below.

circle   special   decide   century   bicycle   notice

What is the difference between the **sounds** made by the '**c**' and the '**s**' in the word '**exercise**'?

_____

STEP 2 (2.5 min) **Practise**

Complete the text using words which contain the letter '**c**' making an '**s**' sound.

| **notice** | **circle** | **sentence** | **centre** |

The teacher said we should put a full stop at the end of the _____.

I did not _____ that I missed one. The teacher drew a _____

where it should be, right in the _____ of my page.

STEP 3 (1.5 min) **Challenge**

What **sound** does the letter '**c**' make in '**special**'?

_____

Add the **endings** below to the word '**special**'. Write the new words.

-ly _____

-ist _____

Time spent: _____ min _____ sec. Total: _____ out of 14   ©HarperCollins*Publishers* 2021

Date: _____

Day of week: _____

Tip Homophones are words which sound exactly the same when spoken but have a different **spelling** and **meaning**. It is important to know the correct spelling and meaning of homophones to avoid confusion.

STEP 1 (1 min) **Review**

Circle the correct **homophone** in each sentence.

There would be no **piece / peace** in the house until everyone had been fed.

They gazed from the hilltop at the beautiful **scene / seen**.

He had to **break / brake** so his bike would not crash into the fence.

Everyone decided to **meet / meat** each other at the park gates.

STEP 2 (2.5 min) **Practise**

Write a sentence for each **homophone**.

medal _____

meddle _____

mail _____

male _____

STEP 3 (1.5 min) **Challenge**

Explain the difference between each pair of **homophones**.

weather and whether _____

_____

missed and mist _____

_____

Date: _____

Day of week: _____

STEP 1 **Review**

 Tip *A near-homophone sounds almost the same as another word.*

Write a sentence for each given word. Use a dictionary to help you.

rain _____

rein _____

reign _____

STEP 2 (2.5 min) **Practise**

Underline the **three pairs** (**six words**) of **homophones** in the sentences below.

I hear that Jessica, who's nine next week, will have a party here.
She said she will invite Martha whose party she could not go to
because she felt ill and weak.

Write a short sentence using each word underlined above.

_____

_____

_____

_____

_____

_____

STEP 3 (1.5 min) **Challenge**

Give a definition for the **near-homophones** given below. Use a dictionary to help you.

affect _____

effect _____

Time spent: _____ min _____ sec. Total: _____ out of 17

STEP 1 (1 min) Review

Each word below should end in '**-sure**' or '**-ture**'. Add the **correct ending** to each word.

struc_____   plea_____   adven_____

lei_____   enclo_____   fea_____

STEP 2 (2.5 min) Practise

Place each word in the correct column in the table.

| television | permission | education | expansion |
| decision | mansion | conclusion | erosion |

'shun' endings	'zhun' endings

STEP 3 (1.5 min) Challenge

Read the passage below. Write the **correct homophone** where errors have been made.

During the weakly training, I could hear someone whose clearly the captain of the team.

_____ _____

There voice was loud and they encouraged others threw the rein and then the missed.

_____ _____   _____ _____

It was a dreary seen but I think the hole team will get a meddle later in the season.

_____ _____   _____

ANSWERS

Test 1
Step 1:
Nouns: Mika, school, bag, watch, bell
Verbs: walked, swung, appeared, looked, ran, arrived, sounded

Step 2:
Ensure each sentence includes one word from each column.
Example: The crocodile ate wonderful food quickly.

Step 3:
The answer should recognise that both words are used to help with describing how a toddler climbs over a wall.

Test 2
Step 1:
he; she; it; they

Step 2:
she; he; it; we / they

Step 3:
Accept appropriate variations on the example below:

Daisy Dormouse looked cute. ~~Daisy~~ **She** was very tiny but ~~Daisy~~ **she** was tough. One day, the dog found ~~Daisy~~ **her** and ~~the dog~~ **it** chased ~~Daisy~~ **her** around the kitchen. ~~The kitchen~~ **It** was a big kitchen and the dog was soon worn out. Daisy managed to give ~~the dog~~ **it** a bop on the nose!

Test 3
Step 1:
theirs; mine; yours; hers

Step 2:
The kite is theirs.   The bike is mine.
The treehouse is yours.   The trainers are hers.

Step 3:
Doug found a newt and says it is now his.   (a newt)
The Smiths won a raffle and say the
main prize is now theirs.   (the main prize)
Suzy gave me some cakes which were
even tastier than mine / ours.   (some cakes)
We liked the house but decided
ours / yours / theirs / his / hers is better.   (the house)

Test 4
Step 1:
summer; log; bus; cold; train; hot

Step 2:
We saw a wonderful, huge **whale**.
I went on **the ride** next to the rollercoaster.
The autumn wind blew hard.
He wore **a hat** on his head.

Step 3:
Accept suitable answers. Examples:
I threw my ball over the fence.
The submarine dived under the waves.
The snow fell on the garden.

Test 5
Step 1:
Note: 'a large bus' and 'James lives here' show neither plurals nor possession. Plural: bats, schools, cats
Possession: Jayden's, man's, child's

Step 2:
Possession: chef's; Jamie's; shop's; Dell's
Plural: holes; fireworks; snakes; streets

Step 3:

foxes	children	churches
puppies	wolves	people

Test 6
Step 1:
Slowly and carefully, she climbed the rockface.
On the other side of the playground, Jess hid behind a large shed.
At the back of the bus, Evan was feeling sick.

Step 2:
Within hours, the snow melted.
During the film, everyone ate popcorn.
Using buckets and spades, we built amazing sandcastles.

Step 3:
Just in time, the eel managed to squirm away.
The eel managed to squirm away just in time.
Following the downpour, fields became huge lakes.
Fields became huge lakes following the downpour.

Test 7
Step 1:
They watched an eagle circling above those trees.
Molly had heard that sound when she slept in her tent.
As soon as they saw the time, they knew they had missed their bus.
This amazing garden belongs to my family, thought Billy.

Step 2:
There are **fewer** / some / those people in the UK than in China.
Chrissy ate a / **an** / several apple yesterday.
You can bring the game to some / those / **my** house to play.
Claudia knew that these / your / **an** incredible jewel had been stolen.
At twelve years old, he set up **his** / those / an car-washing business.

Step 3:
Recognition that 'every' is incorrect because it does not work with 'kittens'. It should be replaced with 'the' (accept 'all the').

Recognition that 'lots' is incorrect because it would need the word 'of' prior to 'children'. It should be replaced by 'many' or 'several'.

Test 8
Step 1:

Sentence	Cause	Time
Wash your hands before you eat your lunch.		✓
They were very cold because they were not wearing coats.	✓	
The dog was chewing the cushion while Zak watched television.		✓
It was a hot day so they took plenty of water with them.	✓	

Step 2:
As the monsoon rain was torrential, they had to take shelter.
So we could make a raft, we searched for days for vines and fallen trees.
Because the rain had been falling heavily, the river was wide and fast.

Step 3:
If; when; after

Test 9
Step 1:
since, time; because, cause; before, time; through, place

Step 2:
We all lay **on** the ground. It was great being **under** the stars. We could see hundreds of them sparkling **in** the night sky. Later we looked **through** the telescope.

Step 3:
Answers will vary. When used as an adverb, 'before' usually follows the noun. For example, We arrived the day **before**.

Answers will vary. When used as a preposition, 'before' is placed before the noun. For example, We got here **before** you. It can also denote place, for example, They sat **before** the roaring fire.

Test 10: Progress Test 1
Step 1:
Sam saw <u>the</u> eagle first. <u>He</u> quickly picked up <u>his</u> binoculars for a closer look.

<u>That</u> noise hurt <u>our</u> ears. Nobody knew where <u>it</u> came from.

Dana lives in <u>that</u> house. <u>She</u> keeps chickens in <u>her</u> garden.

A large cloud hung above <u>their</u> heads and <u>it</u> got bigger and bigger.

Step 2:
Possession: cathedral's; Louie's; shoe's; Miff's

Plural: bells; pizzas; fields; bushes

Step 3:
Responses will vary. Examples:

While <u>walking</u> through the fields, they saw a <u>large bull</u> nearby.

Beneath the <u>hot sun</u>, we wore <u>caps</u> on our heads.

Test 11
Step 1:

Verb	Simple present	Simple past	Present perfect
I	am	**was**	have been
you	**are**	were	have been
he / she / it	**is**	was	**has been**
they	are	**were**	have been

Step 2:
wrote (simple past tense) (Also accept 'were writing', which is the progressive past tense.); paints (present tense); has blasted (present perfect tense); crashes (present tense)

Step 3:
The car <u>has stopped</u> suddenly. Two people <u>have leaped</u> out and <u>(have) charged</u> into the bank. They <u>have been</u> in there for two hours now. The police <u>had arrived</u> within a few minutes of the situation starting.

Test 12
Step 1:
have not; were; those; well

Step 2:
When I **was** on the train I **met** my old friend. We **bought** some lunch and **did** lots of talking. We **have** both been working in London. She said she **does not** (or **doesn't**) like it but I do. In London there **are** many places to visit. They even **have** a big wheel called the London Eye.

Step 3:
Responses will vary but each must use the given words correctly. Examples: I **am** camping and my friends **are** with me.

They **were** camping and there **was** a super camp fire.

Test 13
Step 1:
Note that the answers below do not have a comma before 'and'. While it is not incorrect to add this comma, it is rarely taught or tested in primary schools.

Emmy bought eggs**,** flour**,** butter and milk to make pancakes.

Sam's top three toppings are chocolate spread**,** banana and lemon juice.

Everyone was told to bring cakes**,** old toys**,** books and sweets for the school sale.

Step 2:
<u>As quickly as possible</u>, they ran towards the station.

<u>After their delicious lunch</u>, everybody needed a snooze.

<u>Down at the harbour</u>, Joss could see a huge sailing ship.

<u>Looking at the wonderful scene</u>, Kat remembered the last time she was there.

<u>In the shade of the oak tree</u>, the whole class sat and dozed.

<u>Carefully and silently</u>, Lily reached for the next rope.

Step 3:
Response should acknowledge that the comma has been placed before the end of the fronted adverbial, not after it (the comma should follow 'film').

Response should acknowledge that the comma is not needed after 'saw' as this comes before the first item in the list.

Test 14
Step 1:
What an incredible meal they were served! —————— exclamation
They waited to be seated at the restaurant. —————— statement
Wash your hands before eating, please. —————— command
What food would you recommend? —————— question

Step 2:
Response sentences will vary. Ensure each sentence is grammatically correct. Examples:

The socks were new.	statement
Find your socks, now.	command
Where are my socks?	question
Jess is a good swimmer.	statement
Can Jess swim well?	question
Keep swimming, Jess.	command

Step 3:
Responses will vary. Make sure the same idea is used and the sentence type is changed. Examples: Where is my pencil?

We will see you again soon.

The keys were on the table.

Test 15
Step 1:
S; M; M; S

Step 2:
The dog was asleep when the cat was awake.

We built a snowman because snow had covered the garden.

While they were swimming somebody hid their shoes.

We will go to the art gallery if the museum is closed.

Step 3:

Responses will vary. The first and third clauses can have another main clause added or a subordinate clause. Examples:

Rishi saw the smoke rising from the rooftop. *Or* Rishi saw the smoke and he saw large flames.

As the river flowed it got wider.

A glorious sun was rising above the mountain tops. *Or* A glorious sun was rising and the sky was pink and blue.

When they arrived a large crowd greeted the team.

Test 16

Step 1:

It was a dull day. <u>I wish this rain would pass</u>, moaned Milly. She did not like riding her bike in the rain. <u>Only three more miles until the café</u>, said Mum encouragingly. Despite the rain, Milly now pushed harder on the pedals. She thought of chocolate cake. Almost joyfully she shouted, <u>Come on, I'll race you</u>.

Step 2:

Ensure the inverted commas are around the spoken words, even if not around the commas or question mark.

"Can we have lunch yet?" asked Seb.

"We will stop in 20 minutes," replied Ali.

Her tummy rumbling, Jess said, "I am so, so hungry. I need food."

"We'll stop at the top of this hill as the views are wonderful," promised Ali.

Step 3:

Explanation should recognise that at the end of the spoken words, additional punctuation (such as the question mark or comma) is needed before the closing inverted commas.

Test 17

Step 1:

"It's time to go. Hurry!" shouted Gran. ✓

Lizzie asked, "Who would like to play?" ✓

Step 2:

"Please walk carefully as the floor is wet**,"** said the cleaner.

"Are you going on holiday**?"** asked the bus driver.

When Chloe saw the car, she screamed**, "**Look out!**"**

"You have five tasks today**,"** said the teacher.

Step 3:

Answers will vary. Check for correct use of inverted commas. Examples:

"Can I go on a bike ride?" asked Tommy. (Check for the correct position of the question mark within the inverted commas.)

"I will help you with your homework," Emma told her sister. (Check for the correct position of the comma within the inverted commas.)

Test 18

Step 1:

Apostrophe for contraction	Apostrophe for possession
you can't go	Lena's drink
who would've thought	the cow's grass
we won't be there	Jess's diary
you'll soon find out	a book's cover

Step 2:

cat's; it's; bus' (Accept bus's.)

Step 3:

Responses will vary. Ensure the apostrophe is used correctly. Examples: I played Thomas's (or Thomas') guitar.
We looked at Alisha's painting.

Test 19

Step 1:

P; P; S

Step 2:

car's, SP; children's, PP; people's, PP; fox's, SP; fishermen's, PP

Step 3:

The response should acknowledge that for 'witches' the apostrophe is placed after the final 's' because 'witches' is a plural noun already ending in 's', and that 'geese' is a plural word which does not end in 's', so 's is added.

Test 20: Progress Test 2

Step 1:

Fish and chips <u>are</u> nice together.

Jess <u>doesn't</u> like swimming.

The crowd <u>was</u> huge at the concert.

The plates <u>were</u> in the dishwasher.

Step 2:

The children's club <u>hasn't</u> been open for weeks.

James's homework <u>won't</u> be finished on time.

You <u>shouldn't</u> eat Sophie's sweets.

We're going to my friend's house for lunch.

Step 3:

Chloe shouted**,** "It's a clown!"

"Where are the keys**?**" asked Dad.

Test 21

Step 1:

Prefix 'dis-'	Prefix 'mis-'	Prefix 'un-'	Prefix 'im-'
disappear	misunderstood	unusual	immature
disadvantage	misbehave	unfashionable	impossible
disagree		untidy	imperfect

Step 2:

misorganised – disorganised   dispatient – impatient

unadequate – inadequate   inresponsible – irresponsible

imlogical – illogical   inperfect - imperfect

Step 3:

international – between countries. The prefix inter- means between.

replay – to play something again. The prefix re- means again.

Test 22

Step 1:

joyously; enjoyment; careful; raced

Step 2:

The 'y' is replaced by 'i' before adding '-ly'   happily

The 'e' is dropped before adding '-ing'   facing

The 'y' is replaced by 'i' before adding '-ment'   merriment

Step 3:

basically; gently; angrily; historically

Test 23

Step 1:

A storm is approaching **quickly**.

They **silently** waited for lunch.

Step 2:

'y' ending changed to 'i' before adding '-ous'	'e' ending dropped before adding '-ous'	'u' removed from our ending before adding '-ous'
envious	famous	rigorous
victorious	nervous	humorous

Step 3:
rapidly; running; preferred; noticed; becoming; tapped

Test 24
Step 1:

The reading of a story. ———————— narration

The easing of something or taking it easy. ———— relaxation

An organised activity. ———————— operation

The number of something living somewhere. ——— population

Step 2:
preparation; **investigation**; **formation**; **information**; **animation**; **sensation**

Step 3:
admire – admiration – the 'e' is dropped from the end of the root word before adding '-ation'

occupy – occupation – the 'y' is dropped from the end of the root word before adding '-ation'

exclaim – exclamation – the 'i' is dropped from within the root word before adding '-ation'

Test 25
Step 1:

(fame) – famous   (murder) – murderous   (mountain) – mountainous

Step 2:
outrageous; precious; boisterous; mysterious

Step 3:
miraculous – explanation should acknowledge that the '-le' ending is removed and replaced by 'ul + ous'

mischievous – explanation should acknowledge that the '-f' ending is replaced with 'v + ous'

Test 26
Step 1:
Egypt; pyramids; mysterious; typical

Step 2:
gym; synonym; cygnet; mystery

Step 3:
symbols; hymns; oxygen; system

Test 27
Step 1:

'ch' making a 'sh' sound	'ch' making a 'k' sound
chef	chaos
moustache	character
chauffeur	ache

Step 2:
anchor; machine; chorus; chemist; school; mechanic

Step 3:
school; chemistry; machine; chaos; character; moustache; chauffeur; champagne; quiche

Test 28
Step 1:

Something old such as an old clock ———— boutique

A fancy shop ———— picturesque

A method or way of doing something ———— antique

A beautiful scene or setting ———— technique

Step 2:
mosque – an Islamic place of worship

colleague – a person somebody works with

unique – one off, something there is only one of

©*HarperCollinsPublishers* 2021

fatigued – tired

catalogue – a booklet showing items for sale

intriguing – very interesting

Step 3:
plague – a contagious disease; a large number of insects which cause damage to crops

plaque – a sign on a wall commemorating something or someone; a substance on teeth which can lead to decay if not brushed away

Test 29
Step 1:

A follower of a leader, such as Jesus ———————— disciple

A type of sword ———————— scimitar

A curved moon shape ———————— crescent

The study and investigation of the natural world ——— science

Step 2:
scissors; scene; fascinated; ascending; scientist; muscles

Step 3:
scent – a particular smell
Both are about movement/vertical movement. Ascent means moving up. Descent means moving down.

Test 30: Progress Test 3
Step 1:
mystery; pyramid

gymnasium; oxygen

hymn; typical

Step 2:
science; **a**ntique; **m**eringue; **c**rescent; **c**olleague; **m**osque

Step 3:

	Root word	+ '-ation'
narrative	narrate	narration
forming	form	formation
sensitive	sense	sensation
operational	operate	operation

Test 31
Step 1:
pleasure ✓; measure ✓; closure ✓

Step 2:
erasure; leisure; treasure; enclosure

Step 3:
composure – being calm and controlled

disclosure – telling new or secret information to somebody

Test 32
Step 1:

Everything natural ———— creature

A large bird of prey ———— vulture

A living animal ———— fracture

A break in something ———— nature

Step 2:
structure; furniture; feature

picture; capture; sculpture

Step 3:
Sentences will vary. Example sentences:

mixture	I had cough mixture when I was ill.
departure	A storm delayed their departure by two hours.
moisture	Plants grew well as there was plenty of moisture in the soil.

Test 33

Step 1:

What pupils receive at school ——— musician
Somebody who plays in a band ——— action
A newly thought of thing ——— education
Something being done ——— invention

(matching lines cross)

Step 2:

attention; completion; discussion; tension; expansion; magician

Step 3:

Explanation should acknowledge that words ending in '-mit' have the 't' removed and replaced with '-ssion'.

Test 34

Step 1:

collision; decision; illusion; vision

Step 2:

revise; confuse; intrude; invade; televise; erode

Step 3:

'shun' / '-sion'	'shun' / '-ssion'	'zhun' / '-sion'
extension	profession	conclusion
mansion	procession	explosion

Test 35

Step 1:

disobeying; eightieth; weigh; veil

Step 2:

Answers will vary. Ensure that the sentence makes sense.
Example answers:

neighbour	I saw my **neighbour** at the shops.
they	**They** were buying milk.
reindeer	The **reindeer** crossed the road.
grey	The sky was **grey**.

Step 3:

The answer should acknowledge that 'prey' is something hunted or eaten by another animal, and 'pray' means to say a prayer.

Test 36

Step 1:

build; tongue; favourite; guilty

Her favourite time at school was when they were allowed to get the construction toys out and build whatever they wanted.

Step 2:

guide; antique; question; guards

Step 3:

The 'u' makes a short 'i' sound as in the word 'ink'.

busiest, business

Test 37

Step 1:

circle; special; decide; century; bicycle; notice
The 'c' makes an 's' sound and the 's' makesa 'z' sound.

Step 2:

sentence; notice; circle; centre

Step 3:

The 'c' makes a 'sh' sound.

specially, specialist

Test 38

Step 1:

(peace); (scene); (brake); (meet).

Step 2:

Examples: Everybody in the fun run received a **medal**.

We were told not to **meddle** with the tools in the shed.

The postman dropped off the **mail**.

A stag is a **male** deer.

Step 3:

Responses will vary. Must include reasonable definitions.

'Weather' means the conditions outside, such as wet, dry, hot, cold, rain and sun. 'Whether' can mean a choice between two things – 'whether to have a biscuit or an apple'. It can also mean checking something – 'whether it has happened'.

'Missed' means something has not reached its intended outcome, or somebody or something has not been seen for a while. 'Mist' is a fine cloud of water droplets often gathering over fields or lakes.

Test 39

Step 1:

Each response must use the given word accurately.

The heavy **rain** fell on the large crowd of people.

I held on to the horse's **rein** as I rode across the field.

Queen Elizabeth II has had a long **reign**.

Step 2:

I hear that Jessica, who's nine next week, will have a party here. She said she will invite Martha whose party she could not go to because she felt ill and weak.

Each response must use the given word accurately. Examples:

I can **hear** someone approaching.

Here is the postman.

Whose house is this?

I need to know **who's** done their homework.

There is a whole **week** until my birthday.

We felt **weak** after walking so far,

Step 3:

affect – to make a difference to something by having an effect on it

effect – a change as a result of an action

Test 40: Progress Test 4

Step 1:

structure; pleasure; adventure

leisure; enclosure; feature

Step 2:

'shun' endings	'zhun' endings
permission	television
education	decision
expansion	conclusion
mansion	erosion

Step 3:

During the weekly training, I could hear someone who's clearly the captain of the team. Their voice was loud and they encouraged others through the rain and then the mist. It was a dreary scene but I think the whole team will get a medal later in the season.

STAR WARS®

CLONE WARS

Volume 3

The events in
this story take
place between fifteen
months and seventeen
months after the Battle of
Geonosis (as seen in *Star
Wars: Attack of the Clones*)

STAR WARS

CLONE WARS
VOLUME 3

Last Stand on Jabiim

Dark Horse Books™

colors by **Brad Anderson**

lettering by **Sno Cone Studios & Michael David Thomas**

cover illustration by **Tomás Giorello**

publisher **Mike Richardson**

collection designer **Darin Fabrick**

art director **Mark Cox**

assistant editor **Jeremy Barlow**

editor **Randy Stradley**

special thanks to **Sue Rostoni** and
Amy Gary at Lucas Licensing

STAR WARS®:CLONE WARS VOLUME 3

THIS VOLUME COLLECTS THE FOLLOWING INDIVIDUAL ISSUES: *STAR WARS: REPUBLIC #54-59.*

PUBLISHED BY DARK HORSE BOOKS, A DIVISION OF DARK HORSE COMICS, INC.
10956 SE MAIN STREET · MILWAUKIE, OR 97222
WWW.DARKHORSE.COM   WWW.STARWARS.COM
To find a comics shop in your area, call the Comic Shop Locator Service
toll-free at 1-888-266-4226

FIRST EDITION: ISBN: 1-59307-006-3
3 5 7 9 10 8 6 4 2
PRINTED IN CHINA

illustration by **KEV WALKER**

LAST STAND ON JABIIM

APPROXIMATELY FIFTEEN MONTHS
AFTER THE BATTLE OF GEONOSIS...

"Blood and Rain"
written by **Haden Blackman**
pencilled by **Brian Ching**
inks by **Victor Llamas**

illustration by **TOMÁS GIORELLO**

ONE WEEK LATER...

"Thunder and Lightning"
written by **Haden Blackman**
pencilled by **Brian Ching**
inks by **Victor Llamas**

SHELTER BASE. DAY THIRTY

GENERAL LESKA, WE'VE RECEIVED WORD THAT GENERAL NORCUNA'S FORCES HAVE BEEN WIPED OUT NEAR THE CITY OF CHOAL.

HE'S AMONG THE CONFIRMED DEAD.

THEN I'M NOW THE HIGHEST-RANKING JEDI ON JABIIM.

GIVE ME THE SHORTEST POSSIBLE BRIEFING.

ALTO STRATUS HAS US ON THE RUN THROUGHOUT MOST OF THE NORTHERN HEMISPHERE.

EIGHTEEN JEDI AND NINE THOUSAND CLONE TROOPERS HAVE BEEN KILLED IN BATTLE.

BY THE FORCE...

WE DO HAVE SOME HOPE --

OUR INTELLIGENCE HAS LOCATED STRATUS ON THE RAZOR COAST. IF WE CAPTURE HIM, THE REST OF THE JABIIMI SEPARATISTS MIGHT SURRENDER.

THEN MOBILIZE ALL OF OUR FORCES IMMEDIATELY.

WHAT ABOUT THE SURVIVING PADAWANS WHOSE MASTERS WERE SLAIN?

SEND THEM WITH THE RESUPPLY CONVOY. I'M NOT ORDERING ANY MORE CHILDREN TO THEIR DEATHS.

DAY THIRTY-TWO.

KRA-KOW

JUST A LITTLE WINDED. I'LL BRING UP THE REAR.

YOU OKAY?

THE BATTLE OF JABIIM, DAY THIRTY-SEVEN.

SUPREME CHANCELLOR!

ANAKIN! THANK THE FORCE. WE FEARED YOU WERE DEAD.

NOT YET... HOW DID YOU GET THROUGH TO US?

PERSISTENCE. WE KNOW THE DIRE SITUATION ON JABIIM. ANAKIN, WE NEED YOU TO **LEAD** THE EVACUATION EFFORTS.

I CAN'T **ABANDON** MY FRIENDS, SIR... THEY'LL DIE.

THEY WILL DIE WITH OR WITHOUT YOU, I'M AFRAID. BUT WE CAN'T AFFORD TO LET THE EVACUATION TURN TO CHAOS.

ANAKIN, I'VE PUT MY FAITH IN YOU TIME AND AGAIN. YOU HAVE NEVER FAILED THE REPUBLIC. DO NOT FAIL ME NOW.

YES... YES SIR.

I'LL LEAVE FOR THE MESA IMMEDIATELY.

GOOD. I HOPE TO SEE YOU SOON.

ANAKIN... HE'S RIGHT. YOU NEED TO GO.

THIS ISN'T FAIR...I MY PLACE IS HERE...

THERE'S NOTHING FAIR ABOUT THIS ENTIRE WAR. JUST GO, BEFORE IT'S TOO LATE...

WILL YOU TAKE THIS WITH YOU? IT'S MY MASTER'S **HOLOCRON**...

...I PROMISED HIM I WOULD RETURN IT TO THE TEMPLE. WILL YOU KEEP THAT PROMISE **FOR** ME?

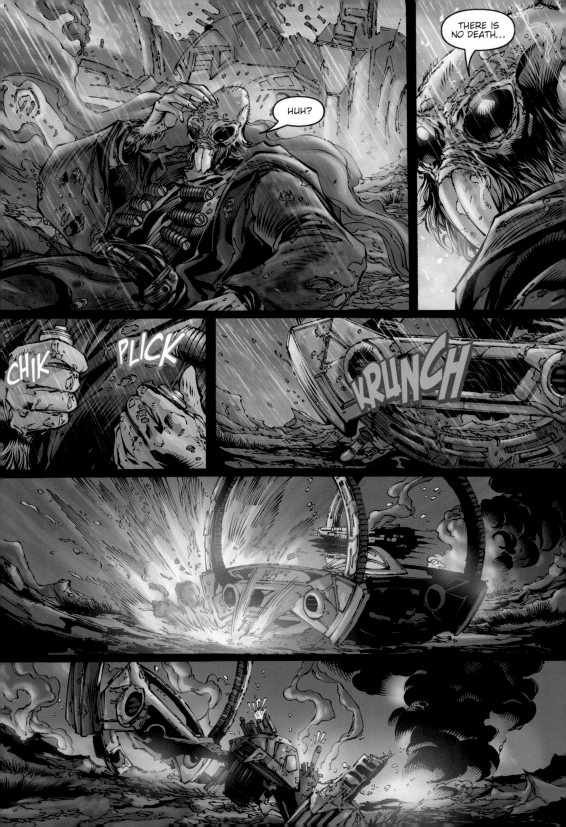

THE BATTLE OF JABIIM.
DAY FORTY-TWO...

CAPTAIN GILLMUNN ... THE REPUBLIC IS FIGHTING ON FRONTS IN HUNDREDS OF SYSTEMS ACROSS THE GALAXY.

OUR FORCES ARE STRETCHED THIN AND WE NEED EVERY TRAINED SOLDIER ON THE FRONT LINES...

WE WILL *NOT* FORGET...

SIR?

NOW THAT WE'RE CLEAR OF THE PLANET, I'M RECEIVING A COMM SIGNAL FROM CORUSCANT. THE SUPREME CHANCELLOR WOULD LIKE A STATUS REPORT.

TELL HIM IT'S OVER..

THE BATTLE OF JABIIM IS OVER. AND WE LOST. WE *ALL* LOST.

YOU LOOK LOST, SKYWALKER.

UH, **MASTER HETT!** I HEARD THAT YOU WERE ON THE FRONT LINES ON METALORN...

WE TOOK METALORN WELL OVER A WEEK AGO.

NEW ORDERS SHOULD BE ARRIVING SOON. UNTIL THEN, **BHAT JUL** AND I ARE BETWEEN ASSIGNMENTS.

VERY LITTLE. THOUGH RUMORS ABOUND.

IN FACT, WE HEARD THAT **YOU** WERE KILLED IN SOME HEROIC LAST STAND ON JABIIM.

GREETINGS, BHAT. ANY NEWS ABOUT THE WAR?

CLEARLY, WE CAN'T TRUST ANYTHING WE DON'T SEE WITH OUR OWN EYES --

-- BUT IT APPEARS THAT THE REPORTS OF OBI-WAN'S DEATH ARE ACCURATE...

Yes...

BHAT, THE ITEM WE DISCUSSED WHEN WE LEARNED ANAKIN WAS ON THE TRANSPORT...

I'LL GET IT, MASTER.

illustration by **JAN DUURSEMA** and **BRAD ANDERSON**

"The Storm After the Storm"
written by **John Ostrander**
pencilled by **Jan Duursema**
inks by **Dan Parsons**

WHAT IS THE STRATEGIC IMPORTANCE OF A LINE? SOMETIMES IT DEPENDS ON *WHERE* YOU'RE STANDING. SOMETIMES IT DEPENDS ON *WHEN* YOU'RE STANDING THERE.

ORDINARILY, *AARGONAR* IS AN UNIMPORTANT PLANET IN AND OF ITSELF. AT THIS MOMENT IN THE CLONE WARS, HOWEVER, IT STRADDLES THE LINE BETWEEN MIGHTY ARMIES BELONGING TO THE *REPUBLIC* AND THE *CONFEDERACY OF INDEPENDENT SYSTEMS*.

THIS PARTICULAR SPOT ON AARGONAR IS NO MORE REMARKABLE THAN THE REST OF THE PLANET. AT THE MOMENT, HOWEVER, IT LIES WITHIN TERRITORY CLAIMED BY THE CONFEDERACY.

A CLAIM DISPUTED BY THE REPUBLIC.

THE REPUBLIC FORCES IN THIS AREA ARE UNDER THE COMMAND OF THE JEDI KNIGHT, *A'SHARAD HETT*, AIDED BY HIS PADAWAN, *BHAT JUL*, AND THE CURRENTLY MASTERLESS *ANAKIN SKYWALKER*.

A'SHARAD COMMANDED THE MOVEMENT OF HIS TROOPS FROM HIS GUNSHIP UNTIL ENEMY FIRE BROUGHT THEM TO GROUND HERE -- BEHIND ENEMY LINES. A LINE DRAWN IN BLOOD ON THE THIRSTY SAND.

A PLACE THAT NOW THREATENS TO BECOME THEIR GRAVES.

HE SHOULDN'T BE DEAD.

YOU SHOULD HAVE BEEN HERE! TOGETHER WE MIGHT HAVE BEEN ABLE TO SAVE HIM!

BHAT JUL AND I WERE CONNECTED THROUGH THE FORCE. I FELT HIM BECOME ONE WITH IT -- AND HE KNEW THAT I WAS THERE WITH HIM.

MY PHYSICAL PRESENCE WOULD NOT HAVE MADE A DIFFERENCE.

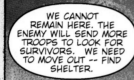

WE CANNOT REMAIN HERE. THE ENEMY WILL SEND MORE TROOPS TO LOOK FOR SURVIVORS. WE NEED TO MOVE OUT -- FIND SHELTER.

WHERE? AARGONAR IS LIKE TATOOINE -- FLAT DESERT AND NO PLACE TO HIDE!

YOU SHOULD LOOK WITH A TUSKEN'S EYES. MY PEOPLE LEARN AT AN EARLY AGE HOW TO READ THE DESERT.

I USED TO TRADE WITH THE JAWAS FOR MY MASTER, WATTO. I *KNOW* ABOUT THE DESERT!

DO YOU KNOW, SKYWALKER, THAT WHEN BANTHAS GATHER NEAR THE CLIFFS IT OFTEN MEANS THERE IS A HIDDEN CAVE? THEY SEEK THE COOL AIR WAFTING UP FROM UNDERGROUND.

IF THE SAME IS TRUE HERE, THEN WE MAY BE ABLE TO TAKE SHELTER THERE.

NOW, QUICKLY. WE NEED TO REACH OUR BASE --

JUST A GUESS, BUT I DON'T THINK OUR SIDE IS WINNING.

SNARKIN' STORM! IF IT WASN'T FOR THIS, WE WOULDA *FINISHED* THEM REPUBLIC MURGLAKS BY NOW!

RELAX. THEY'RE HOLED UP IN VONDAR CANYON. NO WAY THEY CAN REACH THEIR STARSHIPS NOW. SOON AS THE SAND LETS UP, WE FINISH 'EM!

WHAT NOW?

-- AND LEARN HOW OUR FORCES ARE DOING.

"OUR DUTY IS TO FIND A WAY TO REJOIN OUR FORCES."

CONFEDERATE TROOPS ARE APPROACHING, MASTER KI-ADI-MUNDI. NONE OF OUR TRACKING, TARGETING, OR COMMUNICATIONS SYSTEMS ARE WORKING. THE SANDSTORM IS ION-CHARGED. COULD BE WORSE THAN JABIIM!

RALLY THE TROOPS AND PREPARE TO FIGHT ON --

"-- OUR TIME GROWS *SHORT*."

WE DON'T HAVE ENOUGH SHIPS TO FLY INTERFERENCE. WE'LL BE VERY EXPOSED ONCE WE'RE AIRBORNE!

A LEADER *LEADS*, BULTAR SWAN. I MUST SEE HOW THE BATTLE DEVELOPS, AND I CAN ONLY DO THAT FROM THE AIR. BE PREPARED. IF I GO DOWN, *YOU* MUST COMMAND! NOW, TO YOUR SHIP!

I'M NOT CERTAIN IT WAS *WISE* TO TAKE THIS VEHICLE BACK INTO THESE TUNNELS, SKYWALKER! OR TO GO QUITE SO *FAST* THROUGH THEM!

TRUST ME, MASTER!

IF WE WERE ON THE SURFACE, WE'D ALREADY HAVE BEEN SHOT DOWN! THIS *SHOULD* BRING US UP NEAR OUR OWN ARMY!

I HOPE SO. ONE THING, THOUGH --

WE ARE BEING *FOLLOWED*.

IT'S THE *GOUKA*. IT MUST HAVE BEEN ATTRACTED BY THE NOISE OF THE ENGINE!

Obi-Wan's saga will continue in **Clone Wars volume 5!**